# THE MACCABEES

## AN ACCOUNT OF THEIR HISTORY FROM THE BEGINNINGS TO THE FALL OF THE HOUSE OF THE HASMONEANS

ELIAS BICKERMAN

SCHOCKEN BOOKS / NEW YORK

TRANSLATED FROM THE GERMAN BY MOSES HADAS

Manufactured in the United States of America
by H. Wolff Inc., New York

TO T. B.

DEPORTED BY THE GERMANS

PS. 35:17

———

Today the Maccabees are patron saints of Zionist athletic clubs. In the calendar of the Russian peasant they are literally saints; he used to say, and perhaps still does: "Rain on Maccabees [August 1], no fire this year." The word "macabre" is a deformation of the Latin *Machabaei*, and reminds us that the Jewish martyrs were venerated by the Catholic Church. For many centuries, in fact, the Maccabees were regarded by the Christian world as prototypes of holy warriors. Hence the Protestants in their turn appropriated the Maccabees as their forerunners in the struggle against the popish power. In the last century Germans made the Maccabees obscurantists opposing *Kultur*, a stubborn minority resisting the bliss of the National State. Poets are no less divergent. Longfellow's hero would hardly recognize the Judas Maccabaeus of Calderon, and both are very different from the superman pictured by Otto Ludwig.

Any candid interpretation of a historical figure, on whatever level it may be conceived, reveals some

7

facet previously unnoticed. But every presentation trims the hero according to the fashion and the prejudices of the hour. As we look back upon the past we can only judge it according to our own experience and our own needs. In Handel's oratorio Judas Maccabaeus proclaims, "Liberty or Death!" Judah died for freedom, to be sure, but he understood it differently than did Patrick Henry or Handel's audience of 1746. Here the work of the historian begins. With infinite patience, turning his material over and over again, he seeks to restore the figures of the past, as they lived and worked in their own environment. During the space of a century (167–63 B.C.E.) five generations of Maccabees succeeded to the leadership. Instead of judging them as if they were our contemporaries, let us endeavor to be theirs, having as our only advantage that sad knowledge of good and evil which cognizance of subsequent events gives to the historian.

New York, February 1947        E.B.

# CONTENTS

———

# THE PERSECUTIONS

# OF ANTIOCHUS EPIPHANES

## THE PERSECUTIONS

## OF ANTIOCHUS EPIPHANES

———

At the end of the year 167 B.C.E., approximately in December, by order of Antiochus IV Epiphanes, King of Syria and so ruler of the Jews, the Temple on Zion was desecrated and given over to the uses of idolatry. At the same time the law of Moses was rescinded by a decree of the King. Observance of the commandments of the Torah, such as circumcision and the sanctification of Sabbath and New Moon, was made a capital offense. In addition, the Jews were required to worship the gods of the Gentiles. Altars were erected to these gods in every locality, and the populace was commanded to offer sacrifice to the new deities. It was the pig, precisely the animal regarded by the Jews as unclean, that was the most acceptable offering to these gods. Pigs were offered even upon the altar of the Sanctuary at Jerusalem, upon which each day, in early morning and at the approach of evening, offerings had been made to the

God of Israel. The "abomination of desolation" hovered over the Sanctuary and the wrath of God over the people. Never before and never thereafter was the spiritual existence of Israel so imperiled. Was this not the last trial, that Day of the Lord so often proclaimed and threatened by the prophets?

A book has come down to us from this period of persecution, the biblical Book of Daniel. In the midst of these afflictions a seer perceived the significance of the ancient prophecies concerning the world empires, their wars, and the tribulations of the holy people. To him, these prophecies seemed to speak of his own time, and thus he interpreted them for his contemporaries, suiting them to the events during the persecutions of Epiphanes. He felt that the end of time was approaching, and he could see no salvation for the people other than through the direct intervention of God. He knew well enough that the Romans had just driven Epiphanes from Egypt, and that the King was then waging a campaign in the East; yet he refused to think of the possibility, frequently suggested by the prophets, that another earthly power might, in fulfilment of the divine plan, crush the persecutor to earth. Rather would Epiphanes yet conquer Egypt, he foretold: ". . . and there shall be a time of trouble, such as never was

since there was a nation even to that same time"—
until "there came with the clouds of heaven one like
unto a son of man" to rule over the world forever.
The reader of this book knew that supplication and
fast—but never a human act—might alter the course
of events and shorten the period of tribulation.

Daniel's resignation was no accident. Judaism's
cause seemed desperate precisely because the Jews
showed no zeal in its defense. Two centuries later,
when the Roman governor Pontius Pilate had his
standards bearing the image of the emperor set up
in the Temple area, the people went to his head-
quarters at Caesarea and for five days and five nights
besought him to remove the human likenesses from
the Holy City. And when Pilate's soldiers surrounded the crowd with swords drawn, the Jews
bared their necks; they preferred death to acquies-
cence—and Pilate yielded.

But in 166 Jerusalem was filled with monuments
of the pagan cult, and the princes of Jerusalem together with the men of Judea obediently heeded the
will of the earthly ruler. Altars were built before
the doors of the houses and sacrifices were offered
upon them, to make a public display of zeal for the
new paganism. Only a few proved unyielding and
openly transgressed the commandment of the King

for the sake of the commandment of the living God. They were seized, scourged, martyred, and slain.

More numerous were those who sought to evade the order of the King. Without standing forth openly as Jews, they still avoided any participation in the idolatrous rites. In order to lay hold of these, officers of the King journeyed from city to city, coercing the people into open apostasy. They would cause an altar to be erected in the market place, summon the populace, and require them to worship the gods and taste the flesh of the offerings. Many refused, and suffered martyrdom. "They shall stumble by the sword and by flame," says Daniel of them, "by captivity and by spoil, many days."

In the course of the winter of 166 the agents of apostasy made their appearance in the town of Modin, situated upon a hill near Lydda, on the road from Jerusalem to Jaffa. When the first Jew of Modin stepped up to the pagan altar to sacrifice according to the King's will, Mattathias, a priest whose family resided in Modin, sprang out from the circle of bystanders, struck the man down so that his body was stretched out upon the altar, slew the agent of the government, and then pulled down the altar.

In the age of the religious wars, in the sixteenth and seventeenth centuries, the legitimacy of Mattathias' conduct was vigorously debated. His hallowed precedent was held to justify subjects who oppose the authorities in questions of faith. This conception of his deed, which is not without significance even today, would have seemed strange and perhaps dangerous to Mattathias himself. In the speech which his Jewish historian puts into his mouth Mattathias does not dispute the right of the ruler to alter the laws of peoples subject to him; he does oppose an order of the King which is at variance with the revealed commandment of God. The struggle is not one of an individual conscience for freedom of belief; it is rather a conflict between earthly power and the law of the state of God. Mattathias championed the Torah as once Phinehas had done, when he slew Zimri, who had dared worship the Baal of the Midianites (Num. 25). But looked at through the eyes of worldly power, Mattathias' deed was an act of political terrorism. Mattathias and his five sons, John (Yohanan), Simon, Judah, Eleazar, and Jonathan, fled from its punishment into the mountains of Judea.

In those days many in Israel sought out the wilderness. In order not to desecrate the holy covenant they went into the desert with "their sons, and their wives, and their cattle." Such passive resistance by flight

17

was common in antiquity. If an Egyptian peasant was oppressed by taxes, a debtor harried by his creditor, or later a Christian persecuted for his faith, they took this means of eluding the reach of the state, whose organization was not yet so perfected as to lay hold of them. They forsook house and land and lived as wretched vagabonds, as is said of the Maccabees, "after the manner of wild beasts in the mountains." But the state suffered a falling off in revenues as a result, and yielded more and more in the course of time, until finally an amnesty was proclaimed. In the meanwhile, however, agents of the government sought to lay hands upon the fugitives. In 166 B.C.E. a search was instituted in Judea for those who had disregarded the King's command and had hidden themselves away in the wilderness. In this case the task of the police was rendered easy by a Jewish practice which seemed to the pagans the height of superstitious unreason. The Jews, lest they desecrate the day of rest, offered an attacker no resistance on the Sabbath. Thus in 312 B.C.E. Ptolemy of Egypt had been able to take possession of Jerusalem without a blow. Now, too, the fugitives made no attempt to defend themselves on the day of rest; they neither threw stones at the enemy nor walled up the caves in which they had sought safety, but preferred

18

to die in order conscientiously to fulfil the law of God for which they had forsaken their homes.

Mattathias realized the situation: "If we all do as our brethren have done, and do not fight against the Gentiles for our lives and our ordinances, they will soon destroy us from off the earth." Mattathias and his people therefore resolved, not indeed to attack, but at least to defend themselves on the Sabbath day. This rule continued in force until the great uprising against the Romans (66-70 C.E.).

To moderns this interpretation of the fourth commandment seems the "natural" one. But it was far from being so regarded in the days of the Maccabees, as appears most clearly from the fact that the Second Book of Maccabees, which was written in the Diaspora, not only passes over the new resolution in silence but gives especial prominence to the observance of the day of rest by the Jews. It is only in the second century of the Common Era that the rabbis put forward the general principle: "The Sabbath is given to man, not man to the Sabbath."

Even more significant is the fact that Mattathias ventured to interpret the law upon his own authority. In his day this privilege was vested in the High Priest and his council, who governed Jerusalem and Judea. It was the High Priest to whom God had given "authority over statute and judgment, that he might teach His people statutes, and judgments unto the children of Israel." When Mattathias, a man previously unknown, one priest among ten thousand, resolved to interpret the traditional law, to impose his interpretation upon the people, and thus to infringe upon the prerogatives of the High Priest, he raised himself, perhaps without intending to do so, to the position of an opposition government. Hence his resolve constituted a turning point in Jewish history. His measure immediately gave him the authority of a leader. The "community of the pious," a fraternity zealous for the law of God, joined him, and his following was filled with those who fled the evil. Those who had abandoned their homes in order not to depart from the law "either to the right hand or to the left" were united by that very measure which infringed the Torah for the Torah's sake.

Strengthened by these additions, Mattathias determined upon another deed which was pregnant with consequences. Hitherto, like the other fugitives, he had evaded the royal decrees in order to seek a refuge in the desert where he might fulfil the commandments. But now the Maccabees determined to replace passive resistance by active struggle. They made a stealthy and roundabout entrance into the villages and summoned together those eager to fight; with the force thus formed they moved from place to place, destroying the idolatrous altars where they found them, compelling the observance of the Torah by force (for example, they circumcised newborn infants, as many as they found), and smiting apostate violators of the law. Thus, as their historian relates, they liberated the Torah from the hand of the heathen.

But, as is clear from this account, the wrath of the Maccabees was poured over the Jews and not the heathen. The company of the Maccabees was an active minority—Daniel calls them "a little help"— that sought to restore its law to the people. This law was in no sense an innovation, but the revelation of Moses. How came it about that this stiff-necked people backslid from the covenant of their fathers and suffered themselves to be seduced into worship of the pagan deities? Why did the struggle of the Maccabees turn into a civil war within the Jewish people? Why did it not rather become a single-hearted defense of the people against the persecutions of the Syrian king from without?

Until the time of Alexander the Great each Oriental people constituted a disparate unit, clearly differentiated from the others. Even in such a situation cultures inevitably influenced one another: the Book of Proverbs in the Bible, for example, contains many thoughts and aphorisms borrowed from the Egyptian Wisdom Book of Amenemope. Under the domination of the Persians especially, which lasted for two centuries, a great common store of beliefs and ideas developed among the various peoples. But there was no common supranational civilization; a Jew remained a Jew, as an Egyptian remained an Egyptian.

With the Greek conquest of the East (330 B.C.E.), however, the situation changed. From its beginnings Greek culture was supranational, because the Greeks never constituted a unified state. In the East, Greek colonists lost their tribal peculiarities so quickly that the innumerable Greek papyri of the period, discovered in Egypt, show no variations of dialect. The new states in the East were the creation of the Greek race of Macedonia, as Alexander himself was a Macedonian. But their culture was Panhellenic, and was the same on the Nile as on the Euphrates. The Oriental civilizations, on the other hand, were always based upon concepts of folk and religion. A man was born an Egyptian or a Jew, or became such when he forsook his own gods and served new gods. "Thy people shall be my people, and thy God my God," says the Moabitess Ruth to her Israelite mother-in-law when she resolves to follow her.

But Greek culture, like modern European culture, was based upon education. A man became a "Hellene" without at the same time forsaking his gods and his people, but merely by adopting Hellenic culture. Clearchus, a disciple of Aristotle, represents his master as conducting a conversation with a pious Jew and as calling this Jew "a Greek man not only in language but also in spirit." A century later the great geographer Eratosthenes declared that men are not to be distinguished as Greek or barbarian, but rather according to their virtues or their vices.

During the three centuries which we call Hellenistic—that is, the period between Alexander the Great and Emperor Augustus (330 to 30 B.C.E.)—the notion of the "Hellene," like the modern notion of the "European," grew into a concept independent of descent. In Hellenistic Egypt the whole population was officially divided into two classes: the natives, called the "Egyptians," and the immigrants, called the "Hellenes," regardless of their origin. In point of fact, the immigrants were Hellenized with singular rapidity. As early as the third century B.C.E. synagogues in Egypt were dedicated in honor of Greek

23

kings, and the Scriptures were translated into Greek. What could be more Hellenic and more alien to the Orientals than physical culture? But about 220 B.C.E. we find in a Samaritan settlement in Egypt a gymnasium endowed by a Cilician, whose heir was a Macedonian.

In its tendency and in its claim, therefore, Hellenistic culture was universal. To it belonged the mighty of the world and the world's dominion. It was vested with the superiority that the judgment of war constantly reaffirmed. It was open to all. Whether or not to accept this culture was therefore a question of life and death for every people. The nations of the ancient world were confronted by the same problem that confronts the Oriental peoples in the modern world from Tokyo to Cairo, whether to adopt the supranational and therefore superior European culture, or else accept an inferior status, become fellaheen. In antiquity the problem was actually solved by only two peoples, the Romans and the Jews. Other peoples shut themselves off from Hellenism, and its effects upon them were therefore only negative: the native cultures were disintegrated and enfeebled. They lost their upper class, whose connection with the people had been ruptured by the process of Hellenization. The Egyptians, for example, deprived of their upper class, their intellectual elite, for centuries lagged behind the inexorable march of history, and so suffered the fate of enslavement to foreign conquerors. "And there shall be no more a prince out of the land of Egypt."

For Judaism, then, the question of its historical existence or disappearance depended upon its ability to accommodate itself to Western culture. But in the days of the Maccabees, as in the period of Moses Mendelssohn, the law interposed a wall between Jews and non-Jews. Nothing brings people closer together than a common table. But his dietary laws forbade the Jew to taste the food of his non-Jewish neighbor. There is no closer tie than the bond of matrimony. But the Jews told with approval the story of a father who abandoned his own daughter in order to free his brother from a passing attachment to a pagan dancing girl. To a man of the Hellenistic age this "separation from the nations" could be regarded as nothing else than the expression of a Jewish "hatred of mankind." Favorably disposed critics have endeavored to explain the withdrawal of the Jews from history as the consequence of the "bad experience of their expulsion from Egypt," and to exculpate it on such grounds; but no one outside Jewry itself has ever recognized positive merit in the separation. When the Jews declined to associate with pagan slave women, such an attitude seemed an invidious distinction even to a friend of the Jews, who posed the question: "Are they not human beings like yourself?"

To "advanced" Jews, therefore, it seemed imperative to let these bars fall. "In those days," we read in I Maccabees, "came there forth out of Israel lawless men, and persuaded many, saying, 'Let us go and make a covenant with the nations that are round about us; for since we separated ourselves from them many evils have come upon us.' And the saying appeared good in their eyes." "In those days" denotes the reign of the Syrian King Antiochus IV, surnamed Epiphanes (176-163 B.C.E.). The new King entrusted the position of High Priest at the Temple in Jerusalem—and hence the rule over Judea—to men of that same "advanced" party, first to a man who called himself by the Greek name of Jason (about 175-172 B.C.E.), then to Menelaus (172-162 B.C.E.). These Jewish "Hellenists" promptly received royal approval for establishing a Greek community in Jerusalem, and with it permission to erect a gymnasium. In 169, then, a regular Greek city, surrounded by walls and fortified by towers, was founded upon one of the hills of Jerusalem, opposite the Temple Mount. The name of this city is unknown; in our tradition it is referred to simply as Acra, that is to say, the Citadel. Henceforward the Sanctuary was dependent upon this Greek city. This was only natural. The Hellenistic culture, understandably enough, had first affected the upper classes, the Jerusalemites and the priesthood. When the signal went up for the exercises upon the athletic field to begin, it was the priests who hastened to the contests and surrendered their priestly linens for the nakedness of Greek sports. Greek marks of distinction were prized above old-fashioned, native honors. People strove to appear wholly Greek—externally, by removing the marks of circumcision through a painful operation; inwardly, by participating in the games in honor of the foreign gods, and even by contributing money for sacrifices to these gods.

But the leaders of the party understood perfectly well that all this must remain merely a diversion of the upper classes as long as the Sanctuary remained inviolate and as long as the law enjoining "misanthropic" separation continued in force. Like the Emancipation of the nineteenth century, that of the second century B.C.E. must have necessarily led to religious "reform." But nineteenth-century Emancipation could in the end escape this necessity, for

Occidental civilization as a whole had in the interval become secularized.

All of ancient life was carried on within the framework of cult acts whose execution did not entail complete belief. No gymnasium could be without the images of such patron gods of athletics as Heracles and without honorific statues of the kings. Every public act was invariably accompanied by sacrifice and invariably involved prayer. To accept Western culture fully, therefore, there appeared no other alternatives than either to renounce the ancestral religion, to which any participation in the cult of the gods was an abomination, or to transform the ancient law. Many Jews of antiquity chose the first course. Among them, for example, was Tiberius Julius Alexander, nephew of the Jewish philosopher, Philo, of Alexandria. Tiberius pursued a military and administrative career that raised him to the highest stations. Among other things, he was chief of staff to Titus at the conquest of Jerusalem in 70 C.E.

Jason and Menelaus, in the reign of Epiphanes, wished to follow the other course; they desired to accommodate traditional Judaism to the times. Their intention was to preserve those characteristics of the Jewish religion which suited Greek taste—the imageless God, for example—but to remove everything which smacked of separation, of the "ghetto": Sabbath observance, beards, circumcision, and that namelessness of God which was otherwise to be met with only among the most primitive peoples.

Henceforth the Lord on Zion must bear a name which could be communicated to Greek friends who might inquire what manner of God it was that the people of Jerusalem worshipped. In Greek that name was Zeus Olympius. For some time the Jews had been in the habit of calling their God "Lord of Heaven," or even simply "Heaven," as is the regular practice in the First Book of Maccabees. But for the Greeks the Lord of Heaven was Zeus Olympius. In Aramaic the expression was probably *Baal Shemin*, under which title all the peoples of Syria worshipped the ruler of heaven. In this manner the "God of the Jews" was now accepted into the general pantheon. Now He was no longer worshipped in the dim light of the Holy of Holies, but under the open sky, in an enclosure, as was the practice in the most highly revered sanctuaries of Syria and in keeping with the Greek ideal. Even after its transformation, the cult naturally remained aniconic—educated Greeks had long ridiculed the notion that the gods had a human form. But the presence of the Almighty was now symbolized by a "sacred stone" upon the sacrificial altar in the middle of the forecourt of the Temple. All the requirements of the law concerning the sacrificial ritual were rescinded. The pig was now approved as a sacrificial animal: prohibition of its use for sacrifice or food had seemed the most striking mark of Jewish separatism.

After December of 167 B.C.E. sacrifices on Zion were carried out according to the new ritual. Offerings were made to the same God and on the same spot as formerly, but the manner was new and in direct opposition to the old. Moreover, the God of Abraham, Isaac, and Jacob was no longer sole ruler in Jerusalem. Adaptation to the religious customs of the Greeks was impossible without the surrender of monotheism. And so the festivals of Dionysus were celebrated in Jerusalem, and perhaps Athene, too, figured among the new divinities; certainly the deified kings of the ruling dynasty were included.

At the same time the High Priest Menelaus procured a decree from the King prohibiting the Mosaic law and ordering the introduction of pagan customs. Such a measure was in complete accord with the thought of the Greek social reformers, who, since Plato, had always regarded the lawgiver as the creator of social life. According to the historical principles basic to Greek thought, Jewish law was the invention of Moses, enjoined by him upon his followers. If Menelaus now wished to impose his own law upon the people, his conduct could not be regarded as improper. It was these measures that passed into the consciousness of contemporaries and posterity as the "persecutions of Epiphanes." With them the history of the Maccabees begins.

THE UPRISING

JUDAH THE MACCABEE

## THE UPRISING

## JUDAH THE MACCABEE

———

Mattathias' following knew nothing of "historical necessity" and probably very little about the ideas of the reformers. The one thing plain to them was the fact of persecution: the Temple desecrated, the law abolished, and the Jews coerced into a pagan way of life. Against this persecution they defended themselves to the death. When, during 166 (or at the beginning of 165), Mattathias died, leadership devolved, we do not know why, upon the third of his living sons, Judah, surnamed the Maccabee. It is generally assumed that the surname signifies "hammer."

For two years Judah waged guerrilla war like his father, making surprise descents upon the apostates without venturing to attack any walled cities or the tyrant's stronghold in Jerusalem. Now he would appear at Beth Horon (about five hours northwest of Jerusalem), now at Modin, again at Mizpah, or at the Samaritan border. "And he was renowned unto the utmost part of the earth, and he gathered together those who were perishing."

At first the central government paid no attention whatsoever to the Maccabean uprising. It must be remembered that the Seleucid empire extended from Egypt to the Persian Gulf, and that disturbances of this nature flared up constantly at one point or another. The handful of the Maccabees could only be regarded as another robber band on the highways. But in the meanwhile Judah was steeling his company in guerrilla warfare. He also gave it a regular organization by appointing "captains of thousands, and captains of hundreds, and captains of fifties, and captains of tens." It would appear that his force amounted to something more than three thousand men.

It was important for the future course of events that the reform party made no attempt at mustering its strength to put an end, once and for all, to the activity of the marauders. Their failure is easy to understand if we reflect that they belonged to the upper strata of the people, being city dwellers and Jerusalemites, and did not particularly relish chasing after the Maccabees through gorges and over stony hills. The mass of the peasantry, on the other hand, remained secretly devoted to the old faith. Judah ruthlessly extirpated the few in the countryside who followed the reform party, but at the same time he restored freedom of faith to the majority.

Before a battle Judah's company fasted, clothed themselves in sackcloth, rent their garments, and prayed devoutly to the Lord of Hosts: "Behold, the Gentiles are gathered together against us to destroy us. . . . How shall we be able to stand before them unless Thou help us?" Could so devout a prayer arise from the ranks of the reform party to the Zeus Olympius who was the creature of their reason? Surely not. Here, too, the reformers "halted between two opinions." It is significant that when they once sent an offering of money to the Tyrian Heracles, the consciences of the messengers were smitten and instead of using the money for what had been intended, they contributed it in Tyre to the construction of ships.

The new pagans of Jerusalem, the "sons of Acra," sought protection against Judah from the King's officers, whom they assisted moreover with auxiliaries, guides acquainted with the terrain, and the like. Judah defeated the troops that were sent against him, one after the other. When the Syrians were making a slow and laborious ascent to the pass of Beth Horon along the mountain path that led from the coastal plain to Jerusalem, they were suddenly attacked by swarms of Maccabees, routed, and pursued the length of the slope into the lowland. Schooled by this defeat in the hills, another Syrian army took up a position in the plain near Emmaus. This afforded a convenient post for controlling the roads to Jerusalem. Judah made a halt near Mizpah in order to protect the road from Beth Horon to Jerusalem; during the night, under cover of the rough terrain, he led his company to a point south of Emmaus. The Syrian general planned to overwhelm the Maccabees by a surprise night attack. But while the King's troops were looking for Judah's forces in the hills, Judah made an attack at dawn upon the Syrian encampment at Emmaus. Later in the day, when the Syrian troops again approached Emmaus, they saw their camp in flames. They fled to the Philistine country.

The success of Judah can be more readily understood if we reflect upon the difficulties that guerrilla warfare in a hill country presents even to modern regular troops. The Seleucid armies were composed largely of contingents of auxiliaries from various cities and peoples; the professional soldiery was employed only for more important enterprises.

It was now, in the fall of 165, that Judah's successes began to disturb the central government. He appears to have controlled the road from Jaffa to Jerusalem, and thus to have cut off the royal party in Acra from direct communication with the sea and thus with the government. It is significant that this time the Syrian troops, under the leadership of the governor-general Lysias, took the southerly route, by way of Idumea. They encamped at Beth Zur, a fortress about thirty kilometers south of Jerusalem (whose remains have recently been excavated) that was the key to Judea from the south. This new tactic proved correct. Judah was forced to quit his hiding place in the hills and hurry southward. According to Jewish historical tradition, he then and there defeated Lysias. But certain other documents which happen to be preserved indicate that the situation was much more complicated than the Jewish historians represent it to have been. We see that the Maccabees sent deputies to Lysias to negotiate an understanding. Lysias promised to intercede for them with the King, if they would maintain their "good will towards the state." Menelaus, officiating High Priest and head of the reform party, intervened in the negotiations and appeared as mediator between the King and the Jews. A Roman embassy, probably en route to Antioch, took the Jews' part and persuaded them to formulate their demands quickly so that they themselves might present them to the King. Thus it appears that all parties were concerned to make peace between the government and the insurgents. In point of fact, Epiphanes was at the moment engaged in a serious war in the East, the imperial treasury was again empty, and the question of whether the Jews would eat in accordance with or in opposition to their dietary laws must now have seemed of little consequence to the government.

And so Epiphanes resolved to call a halt to the persecutions. In a proclamation to the Sanhedrin and the Jewish nation, he declared that he had been informed by Menelaus that the Jews who had fled from their homes—that is, those loyal to the ancient faith, amongst whom were the Maccabees—desired to return to their legal abodes. Exemption from punishment was guaranteed all who returned by March 29, 164 B.C.E., and in addition the assurance was given that the Jews would be permitted "to use their own food and to observe their own laws as of yore." The persecution was thus ended.

The edict makes no mention of the Maccabees, by

as much as a syllable. It is represented as an act of royal grace, instigated by Menelaus. But such an interpretation could not conceal the true state of affairs. The cessation of the persecutions signified the defeat of Menelaus, who had been their instigator, and the victory of the Maccabees—something that must have seemed unbelievable to contemporaries. David had again overcome Goliath. Only a year before the prophet Daniel could see no help except through a miraculous intervention of God. And yet Judah had won his victory with casual irregulars who were often lacking in such essential arms as sword and shield. How could the issue be interpreted as other than explicit confirmation of the leadership which the Maccabees had assumed?

From the beginning Judah comported himself as the lawful leader of his people. He put into force the law (Deut. 20:5-8) according to which a man who had built a house or betrothed a wife or planted a vineyard or was fainthearted was released from service. His people conscientiously separated first fruits and tithes, but these could only be offered in the Sanctuary, and the Sanctuary was still in the hands of the reform party. Epiphanes' restoration of freedom of conscience had only brought an end to the persecutions, but not to the rule of Menelaus and his friends. It was not to be expected that they would voluntarily surrender their position.

Judah therefore determined to wrest their rule from them by force. The tradition unfortunately leaves us in the dark as to where he and his people spent the summer of 164. It can be assumed that after the amnesty the majority of his men returned to their abandoned homes and fields. Hence it is probable that Judah re-enters history only toward the end of autumn, when work on the farm was finished.

At the end of 164, about the beginning of December, he again assembled "the entire host" and made a sudden descent upon Jerusalem. To understand that such a surprise attack could promise success, it must be remembered that in 168 the central government had pulled down Jerusalem's city walls; the intention was to make the city completely dependent upon the citadel of Acra. It was this that made it possible for Judah, only four years later, to take possession of Jerusalem so easily.

The first act of the conqueror was the purification of the Holy City of all traces of idolatry and the restoration of the service of God in the Temple. According to the Jewish calendar, it was Kislev 25, precisely three years after the reform party had offered the first pagan sacrifice upon the altar, that Judah again carried out, in early morning, the prescribed Tamid sacrifice in the ancient usage. "And all the people fell upon their faces, and worshipped, and gave praise unto heaven, to him who had prospered them." For eight days the rededication of the purified altar was celebrated. Then "Judah and his brethren and the whole congregation of Israel ordained, that the days of the dedication of the altar should be kept in their seasons year by year for eight days, from the twenty-fifth day of the month Kislev, with gladness and joy." This celebration, which is the model for the annual festivals of dedication in all churches, is Hanukkah, a word that literally signifies "dedication." But this name can be documented only from the first century C.E. Originally the festival was called "Tabernacles (*Sukkot*) of the month of Kislev,"—so, for example, in an official communication from the Palestinian to the Egyptian Jews, dated 124 B.C.E.

By instituting this festival Judah and his people declared themselves the true Israel. Their act was one of far-reaching significance, for all previous festivals were prescribed in Scripture. Never had a festival been instituted in Israel by human hand.

Even the restoration of the Temple after the Babylonian Exile had not been solemnized by the establishment of a day of commemoration. Judah's measure was therefore an innovation without precedent. On the other hand, it was in complete accord with the usage of the Gentiles. Among the Greeks it was usual for a generation, when it regarded an event in its own history as important, to believe it should be commemorated for all time. Thus Judah imitated the practice of his enemies, but at the same time incorporated it into Judaism. This was the first step along the path which was to constitute the historic mission of the Hasmoneans—the introduction of Hellenic usages into Judaism without making a sacrifice of Judaism. No one any longer celebrates the Greek festivals that served as Judah's example. But the eight-branched candelabrum, a symbol, again, that imitates a pagan usage, is lighted on Kislev 25 the world over, in countries Judah never knew about, in Sidney as in New York, in Berlin as in Capetown. "And He saved them from the hand of him that hated them, and redeemed them from the hand of the enemy."

Master now of Jerusalem, Judah at once built high walls and strong towers about Mount Zion, quartered troops in the fortifications to protect the

Temple, and then fortified Beth Zur, which, as has been mentioned, protected the road to Jerusalem from the south. Thus, at the beginning of 163, Judah was master of Judea; only Acra remained as refuge and citadel for those loyal to the King.

We do not know why the group about Menelaus remained so inactive throughout this entire period. Apparently the garrison in Acra was too weak to act independently and the central government was, as usual, little concerned with the affairs of Judea. Moreover, at this time Epiphanes suffered a serious reverse in Persia when he attempted to plunder an Oriental sanctuary in the hill country, and was lying sick at Ispahan.

At the end of the winter of 163 B.C.E. Epiphanes died at Ispahan. About the same time Judah began the siege of Acra, already employing in this operation the best equipment of the great armies of that period, siege towers and battering-rams of various types. An unknown fugitive four years before, Judah was now, though without office or title, ruler over the Jewish nation. From Acra urgent dispatches went out to the central government. The reform party complained, with perfect justice, that the government was again leaving them, the group loyal to the King, in the lurch. "We were willing to serve thy

45

father," the messengers said to the new king, Antiochus V Eupator, "and to walk after his words, and to follow his commandments. For this cause the children of our people besieged the citadel, and were alienated from us, and as many of us as they could light on they killed, and spoiled our inheritances."

At the head of the new government there stood as regent the same Lysias with whom Judah had negotiated a year previously and who had promised the Jews his good will if they would continue loyal. But in the meanwhile Judah had broken the peace and had taken advantage of the amnesty granted him to make himself master of Judea. The court at Antioch determined to dispose of the Maccabees once and for all.

In the summer of 163 Lysias himself marched at the head of an army of professional soldiers through Idumea to Jerusalem in order to raise the siege of Acra. His way was barred by the citadel of Beth Zur, which Judah had in the meanwhile occupied. Lysias directed the siege of this fortress, and Judah, obliged to hasten to the assistance of his outposts, was forced to interrupt the siege of Acra. This was Lysias' first success. Near Beth Zechariah, halfway between Jerusalem and Beth Zur, where the hills merge into a plateau that permits the deployment of larger battle formations, Judah one morning came upon Lysias' superior army, which included cavalry, and even thirty-two elephants, arms that were wholly wanting to the Maccabees. The rising sun was reflected in the gilt and brazen shields of the Syrian heavy infantry, so that "the mountains shone therewith, and blazed like torches of fire." Judah's brother, Eleazar, vainly immolating himself in an effort to save his people, rushed into the ranks of the enemy and attacked the largest of the elephants, upon which he naively supposed the young king to be riding. The beast, transfixed, fell, crushing the hero. Judah's army was defeated and Beth Zur capitulated.

The royal army now reached Jerusalem unhindered and laid siege to the fortified Mount Zion, where Judah and his people had taken refuge. In ancient times, before the use of explosives, every wall and every tower was an obstacle to the attacker. The besiegers therefore preferred to starve out rather than storm a besieged fortress. It was the summer of a Sabbath year, in which, according to biblical law, nothing had been planted. Hence there were no considerable supplies in Zion. Judah's troops dispersed, each man to his own home. Only a small company of the most faithful remained shut up in Zion under Judah's leadership. Judah's life was in any case forfeit. Moreover, we may surmise, he was firmly convinced that the God of Abraham, Isaac, and Jacob would not forsake him. In his desperate situation, therefore, Judah awaited a miracle, and the miracle came about. Expressed in untheological language, Judah's tenacity made it possible to expect a favorable turn in the situation, which, in the unforeseeable complications of life, might at any time take place.

The deliverance of the besieged Maccabees on Mount Zion came about as result of Epiphanes' last act on his deathbed in Persian Ispahan. When the King marched to the east he had left the guardianship of his son and successor, a minor, to Lysias, who after the death of the King assumed the regency. But on his deathbed Epiphanes had appointed another general, named Philip, as regent of his realm. And so it came about, approximately in February of 162, that while Lysias was occupied with the siege of Zion, he received word that Philip was approaching Antioch at the head of the army of the east to secure the overlordship for himself. Lysias found it necessary to withdraw in great haste, and so quickly made a peace with the beleaguered Judah.

Formally considered, the "peace" amounts on the

one hand to a capitulation on the part of Judah, and on the other, to a remission on the part of the King. In actuality, its basis was an understanding between Lysias and Judah which was tantamount to a restoration of the conditions that had obtained in Judea prior to Epiphanes. The King's remission was addressed to Lysias, and solemnly proclaimed renunciation of the policy of Epiphanes. "As for our Jewish subjects," the new King wrote, "we understand that they object to our father's project of bringing them over to Hellenism, preferring their own ways of life and asking permission to follow their own customs," and he was of the resolve "that the subjects of the realm should live undisturbed and attend to their own concerns." He agreed "to give them back their temple and to permit them to live after the manner of their ancestors."

A year earlier the government had consented to *tolerate* the Jewish religion; now the *dominion* of the Torah was fully restored. According to the decree of 163, those Jews who wished to do so might give obedience to the Jewish law. The new decree of 162 again obliged the entire people to observe this law. This marked the consummation of the victory of orthodox Judaism. For centuries thereafter the Jews celebrated the recurrence of this day (Shevat

28) "upon which King Antiochus withdrew from Jerusalem."

The consequences of the peace of 162 were two-fold. For one thing, it marked the end of the reform party. Its chief, the former High Priest Menelaus, was executed upon the King's orders, "for that he was the cause of all the evil in that he persuaded Epiphanes to abolish the ancestral constitution of the Jews." This was the ground on which the verdict was based. The remaining partisans of reform, who continued to find refuge in the Acra, had in the meanwhile lost all touch with Judaism. The reformers had now become apostates.

On the other hand, the task of the Maccabees also seemed to have been completed. The government had deserted the reform party, traditional Judaism had been recognized as alone valid, and the conditions which had obtained before the promulgation of Epiphanes' measures were thus restored. The rebellion of the Jews now seemed pointless and at an end. "Now therefore let us give the right hand to these men, and make peace with them, and with all their nation; and let us settle with them that they be permitted to walk after their own laws, as aforetime; for because of their laws which we abolished were they angered, and did all these things." This opinion of the young King's counselors proved correct. Judah was deserted by his partisans. The government appointed a new High Priest, a member of the previous high-priestly family called Jakim, who then Hellenized his name into Alcimus. The government even caused an assembly of scribes to be convoked so that it might confirm, after exhaustive investigation, that Alcimus was in fact the legitimate prince. The *Hasidim,* the "Pious," a group known for the strictness of its faith and who had been the first to join Mattathias, these very *Hasidim* were now the first to recognize Alcimus. From this time forward, supported by a royal guard, Alcimus ruled over Judea, and his power was so secure that he could without misgivings cause the execution of sixty of the "Pious" who had shown themselves rebellious. Once again the burnt offering for the reigning king was daily offered upon Zion.

At first Judah again retired into the mountains. But when a new revolution took place in Antioch—Antiochus V was overthrown by his cousin, Demetrius I—Judah took advantage of the occasion to reappear in Jerusalem. He took possession of the Sanctuary and even prevented Alcimus from approaching the altar. Judah's supporters maintained that Alcimus had "voluntarily polluted himself" in the time of Epiphanes; that is, without being compelled to do so, he had participated in pagan festivals and sacrifices. Was such a man now eligible to perform the service of God? The question was one of conscience, fought out by zealots and moderates, similar to the question which later arose among the early Christians during the time of persecutions: Can there be forgiveness for apostasy? We know that the various answers to this question led to numerous schisms within the Church and to reciprocal excommunications. It is therefore not surprising that Judah and his followers refused to recognize Alcimus, even after an assembly of sages convoked by the government had pronounced in favor of Alcimus' legitimacy.

This time the cleavage in the Jewish people was quite different from that in the days of Epiphanes. The struggle no longer concerned the validity of the Torah but whether or not Alcimus was justified in functioning as High Priest. As in the case of analogous divisions in the Church, the preponderant majority inclined to the latitudinarian view and recognized Alcimus. The former friends of the Maccabees were now transformed into enemies, "apostates." Civil strife began anew. Judah again marched forth. He swept through all the territory of Judea, taking vengeance upon his enemies and punishing the "apostates" who were worse than pagans in his eyes.

Twice Alcimus went to the royal court to request the government's help against the Maccabees, "who are keeping up the feud and stirring sedition; they will not let the kingdom settle down in peace." But Demetrius was entirely taken up with other difficulties, especially with the uprising of the satrap Timarchus, who, with Roman support, had wrested Mesopotamia from the King. Finally the King sent out one of his generals, Nicanor, with orders to take the Maccabees captive. Nicanor first sought to lay hands on Judah by cunning; but when the attempt miscarried, he marched his troops out of Jerusalem into the neighborhood of Beth Horon, where he was joined by troops from Syria. He himself led a levy of Jews loyal to the King out of Jerusalem. Because his troops were Jewish, he was constrained, much against his will, to abandon his intention of attacking Judah on the Sabbath. This was approximately in the month of March, 161 B.C.E.

The political situation had rapidly changed. It was only four years before that the government had punished the observance of the day of rest with death, and those wishing to hallow the Sabbath had sought help and refuge with Judah. Now they marched side by side with pagan soldiers in the attempt to capture Judah and send him to his death. At Adasa, northwest of Beth Horon, an hour and a half north of Jerusalem, where the road narrows as it passes through the hills, the opposing forces encountered one another. Judah's troops again proved far superior to the city levies. Nicanor fell on the field of battle and his army fled. Judah besieged Jerusalem and the Sanctuary a second time, and again had the day of his victory (Adar 13) entered in the calendar of festivals. This amounted to a demonstration that Judah and his followers represented the true Israel. For the first time in the history of Jacob a day in a war between brothers was declared a joyous festival. This example was later followed by the Pharisees, who upon occasion abused the function of festivals by instituting anti-Sadducee memorial days. All of these festivals, including the Day of Nicanor, have been forgotten. But the historian must point out that by instituting festivals of this nature Judah no less than the Pharisees was consciously or unconsciously imitating the example of the Greeks.

The victory over Nicanor in March 161 made Judah master of the country once again. He was not the only rebel in the empire. The prince of Greater Armenia, the governor of Commagene, and, above all, Timarchus, satrap of Media and Babylonia, had renounced their allegiance to King Demetrius I. These defections were facilitated by the Roman Senate, which refused to recognize Demetrius, supported his opponents, and finally concluded an alliance with Timarchus.

What did Judah know of Rome? The First Book of Maccabees represents him as having heard of the great reputation of the Roman people, "that they were valiant men, and that they were friendly disposed towards all who attached themselves to them, and that they offered friendship to as many as came unto them." That was enough for him. An exact knowledge of the details of a situation is often unnecessary, frequently even a hindrance, to resolute action. Judah knew that a Roman embassy had once before helped him (in 164 B.C.E.); he knew too that "whomsoever they will to succor and to make kings, become kings; and that whomsoever they will, do they depose." He therefore sent emissaries to Rome. They were well received and the Senate, which, as we have seen, was anxious to cause Demetrius I all possible difficulty, approved the treaty that was concluded, not, to be sure, with Judah and his brothers, but with the "nation of the Jews." "When the Jews rebelled against Demetrius I," an ancient historian writes, "and sought the friendship of Rome, they were the first of all Oriental peoples to receive a grant of freedom; the Romans were generous in disbursing what was not theirs." In any case, for the first time since the Exile the Jews were recognized as an independent power, and by the very people that ruled the world.

Christian theologians have often wondered at the fact that Judah, who was so zealous in the service of the Lord, made a treaty with and sought security through a pagan power, despite all the admonitions of the prophets. It must be said that there is ground for such wonder. The Maccabees had again taken a step that brought them nearer to the pagan world; they had again accommodated devout Judaism to the ways of the nations.

It may be argued that the Roman alliance, which was Judah's greatest success, became the immediate cause of his downfall. The Seleucid government could look on calmly at the occasional successes of a guerrilla chief, in expectation of a favorable moment for delivering a blow. But when Judah became a protégé of Rome, it seemed essential to act at once. Judah's emissaries returned to Jerusalem towards

the end of the summer of 161. In the first month of
the following spring, as soon as the rainy season was
ended, the King's general Bacchides, accompanied
by Alcimus and at the head of a regular army, moved
through Galilee towards Jerusalem. As always, the
professional soldiers were qualitatively far superior
to the Maccabean irregulars. When the Syrians approached, the greater part of the Maccabean levy,
which amounted to three thousand men, fled. Only
eight hundred remained with Judah, and "he was
sore troubled in heart." Friends advised him to avoid
the battle, and their counsel was undoubtedly stra-
tegically sound. But he preferred death in battle,
and fell fighting. "All Israel made great lamentation
for him and mourned many days, and said: 'How is
the mighty one fallen, the savior of Israel!'"

Israel quickly forgot Judah. In the Talmud he is
nowhere mentioned. In *Megillat Antiochus*, a post-
talmudic (and quite spiritless) account that was read
at the Hanukkah festival in the Middle Ages, Mattathias and his grandson, John Hyrcanus—but not
Judah—are the principal figures. It was only during
the Middle Ages, thanks to the Hebrew compilation
called *Josippon*, composed on the basis of the writings of Josephus, that Judah again became a hero
for the Jews. The Christian world, which had taken

the Books of Maccabees into their Holy Scripture, meanwhile honored Judah as a paragon of knighthood. Even today the statue of Judah may be seen in the principal market place of Nuremberg. His figure, along with those of eight other heroes (three pagans, three Jews, three Christians), decorates the *Schöne Brunnen* (1385), a masterpiece of the age of chivalry.

# ON THE ROAD TO INDEPENDENCE

———

Judah fell in April 160 B.C.E. After his death "the lawless put forth their heads in all the borders of Israel, and all they that wrought iniquity rose up." The partisans of Judah were tracked down everywhere and large numbers were executed. A system of garrisoning instituted by the Syrians provided for the peace and order of the country. Jonathan, Judah's brother and successor, again became the simple chief of a band, and sought refuge now in the wilderness of Tekoa and now in Trans-Jordan. Not much more can be told of his deeds during this period than an attack upon an Arab wedding procession to avenge the death of his brother John. Finally, about 156, he grew weary of the life of an outlaw. He too made his peace with the government, gave hostages for his good conduct, and received Michmash, a place west of Jericho, as his place of residence. Here "he began to judge the people," that is to say, he was recognized by the government as sheik of the village. In ancient times, and even later, this was the lot that many an Oriental leader of a troop earned in the decline of his life; in this way he was assured a secure benefice. "And the sword ceased from Israel."

Eight years elapsed after the death of Judah before the Maccabees again entered history. It was the Syrians who aroused Jonathan from his slumbers in Michmash. In 152 B.C.E. a pretender called Alexander Balas arose against the reigning king, Demetrius I, the conqueror of Judah. Alexander Balas landed at Acco and its garrison went over to him. Demetrius was in great straits, for the Roman Senate had recognized Alexander, and the kings of Egypt, Pergamum, and Cappadocia supported him. This made it extremely difficult, if not impossible, for Demetrius to obtain soldiers abroad. The King required reliable troops immediately. What could be more natural than to turn to his warlike Jewish subjects and there enlist the necessary warriors? Twenty centuries ago the highland Jews of Palestine were rough peasants and shepherds who had grown up in an inhospitable country; they were known for their boldness and ruthlessness in war, and like the Arabs they terrified neighboring agricultural countries by their inroads. As soon as they gained a footing on the coast under Jonathan, we find pirates among them. All in all, they were excellent soldiers, loyal to their oath of fealty, whose only inconvenience was their numerous "superstitions," as for example the apparently stupid custom of observing complete rest every seventh day, a habit whose purpose no Greek was able to fathom.

But an inexcusable blunder on the part of the central government had left Jewry at this juncture with no legitimate prince. After the death of Alcimus in the spring of 159, no successor had been named. There was only one man who commanded sufficient authority among the Jews to muster an army for Demetrius I. This was Jonathan, Judah's brother and heir. Demetrius gave Jonathan full power to collect troops.

Jonathan naturally used the opportunity first to secure his own position—he occupied Jerusalem and fortified Zion anew. Syrian garrisons continued only in Acra and in Beth Zur. Naturally, too, Alexander Balas now sought to draw the Jewish leader over to his side. Jonathan demanded his price, and it was given him. At the Feast of Tabernacles in 152 B.C.E. he clothed himself, by the authority of Alexander Balas, in the sacred vestments of the High Priest.

Judah had fought bitterly against the High Priest Alcimus because he was "polluted." Eight years later Jonathan raised himself to the position of High Priest, despite the fact that he was not a member of the Zadokite family to which the office appertained. For the priest to obtain his position from the secular power was a Greek custom. Once again those who fought for the Torah accommodated the law to Gentile practices, while the legitimate High Priest (by right of descent) performed the service in a rump temple in Egypt.

Jonathan's fantastic rise in the few months of the autumn of 152 B.C. from petty chieftain to High Priest of the Temple in Jerusalem and prince in Israel ushers in a chapter in the history of the Maccabees which, except for the identity of the family, has little in common with the previous course of their destiny. Judah's lifework had been to prevent the threatening Hellenization of Judaism and the surrender of the Torah. He succeeded, and gave his life to his success. Jonathan and his successors, his brother Simon and Simon's descendants, will now seek to accommodate Hellenism to Judaism. Under them Judea becomes a Hellenistic principality.

This development began with Jonathan's becoming involved in international politics. Perhaps this involvement was at first a matter of necessity. As prince of Judea he was forced to choose among the pretenders who throughout his entire reign competed for the crown of Syria. But this meant that for the first time since the destruction of the First Temple and the Babylonian Exile (586) Judea became an active member of the family of nations.

Jonathan's first task was to maintain himself. This required that he watch the political currents and keep in touch with the pagan princes; but it also meant that he had to sacrifice the blood of Jews for the cause of one or the other of the pretenders. He became a Seleucid official, a *strategos* and governor of a province; he received a court title and wore the purple reserved for the "friends of the king." At one time he sent the government three thousand men to suppress an insurrection in Antioch. They set the city on fire, slew everyone who fell into their hands, and plundered at will. It can be imagined with what relish these peasants and shepherds pillaged the pagan city.

Jonathan's second endeavor was to secure his position in Jerusalem. He had many enemies in Judea, of course, who took every opportunity to complain of him to the government. The Greek city of Acra and its citadel remained a constant threat to his rear.

At one time he sought to take it by force, another time to negotiate for it with the government. But the kings in Antioch, as soon as they came to power, held fast to this stronghold by which they were able to control Jonathan.

Finally he proceeded to round out the boundaries of his principality; it is significant that what he sought first of all was access to the sea. His brother, who also obtained official preferment and was promoted to the governorship of the (at that time) non-Jewish coastal region, took advantage of the opportunity to place a Jewish garrison in the pagan city of Jaffa, in order to forestall the city's going over to a pretender to the throne.

It is superfluous to describe in this place the campaigns and political combinations in which Jonathan, and after his death his brother and successor, Simon, engaged. (Jonathan was taken captive and murdered at the end of 143 by a Syrian pretender.) They fought battles as *condottieri* now of one and now of another of the Seleucids against their opponents, and always found a reason to shift their allegiance as circumstances demanded. Meanwhile they strengthened the position of their house in Judea. Thus they succeeded in getting into their power all important fortresses, such as Beth Zur,

Gezer, and, finally, Acra in Jerusalem—this last on Iyar 23 (about May) 141. During the same period and by the same means, veering between kings and counterkings, many other leaders succeeded in establishing principalities in Syria.

But in two respects the work of Jonathan and of Simon was different from that of their rivals. For one thing, they preceded the others, who came up in the following generation. Next, and in particular, the Maccabees not only established their personal authority but also extended the power of their people. The basis of their rule was national, or more properly, religious. When Simon won Gezer or Acra, he expelled the pagan inhabitants, purified the place of "pollution," and settled it with Jews.

The results of Jonathan's and Simon's activity may accordingly be summarized somewhat as follows: In 152, when Jonathan was installed as High Priest, the boundaries of Judea were the Jordan and the Dead Sea on the east; the meridian of Modin (approximately) on the west; Beth Horon and Bethel to the north; and in the south, Beth Zur. Jonathan added to this three districts of southern Samaria, and also Lydda and Ekron. Simon acquired the great plain, the seacoast from Jaffa to Ascalon, and Hebron in the south. In fifteen years the extent of the area subject to Jerusalem was approximately doubled; not only the hill country but the fertile plain now became Jewish and Jerusalem was provided with its harbors.

Their political success consisted in the emancipation of the Jews from the rule of the Seleucids. In May 142 Simon obtained Israel's complete freedom from tribute. "Therefore was the yoke of the heathen taken away from Israel." Public documents began to be dated according to the years of Simon. A year later the Hellenistic city and the citadel in Jerusalem, Acra, was taken. In the year 139 Simon received the royal privilege of striking (copper) coins in his own name. On Elul 18 (about September) of the preceding year (140 B.C.E.) "in a great congregation of priests and people and princes of the nation, and of the elders of the country," it was determined that Simon should be "their leader and High Priest for ever." Heretofore the legal basis for the power of the Maccabean princes had been royal appointment. Now the rule of Simon and of his successors rested upon the decision of the people itself; hence Simon assumed the new title, "Prince of the People" (Ethnarch). But lest the people in its fickleness change its mind, it was also resolved that no one should be permitted to alter this law or to convoke assemblies without Simon's consent.

These various successes the Jews owed not so much to their own strength as to the adroitness of their leaders, Jonathan the "Sly" (so is his nickname *Aphphus* probably to be interpreted) and his brother, the Ethnarch Simon. Jonathan and Simon made their conquests as *condottieri* of the pretenders to the Syrian throne, whose partisans threw the gates of the rebellious cities open to them. Only in such a manner was it possible for Jonathan, for example, to subjugate a city like Gaza—which would ordinarily have required a siege of years—merely by devastating the surrounding countryside. This signified only that the city had attached itself to King Antiochus VI, who was represented by Jonathan, and not at all that it had surrendered to the Jews. Although Jonathan and Simon after him continued to hold the cities they had won, garrisoning them for security, it was clear that as soon as the dynastic struggles of the Seleucids ended they would have to restore their conquests to their legitimate suzerains. Jonathan and Simon gambled on the wars of the pretenders never ending. On the whole, they were quite right, but a temporary consolidation of Seleucid power nevertheless robbed the Maccabees of their gains, and forced John Hyrcanus, the son and successor of Simon, to revolutionize the foreign policy of his house and hence also the internal structure of the princedom.

In the year 139 there appeared a new pretender in Syria, Antiochus VII Sidetes, son of that Demetrius I who had crushed the insurrection of Judah the Maccabee. Antiochus was forced to wage war against Tryphon, a general who had proclaimed himself king and had removed the former ruler, Antiochus VI, an illegitimate grandson of Epiphanes.

While yet upon his way to Syria, Antiochus VII confirmed all of Simon's former privileges and in addition granted him the right to strike coins of small denomination "for thy country with thine own stamp." But when he arrived in Syria he immediately made a demand upon Simon either to surrender the cities outside Judea, such as Jaffa and Gezer, and, significantly, Acra in Jerusalem, or to make a single payment of a thousand talents of silver in compensation. Simon replied: "We have neither taken other men's land, nor have we possession of that which appertaineth to others, but of the inheritance of our fathers; howbeit, it was had in possession of our enemies wrongfully for a certain time. But we, having the opportunity, hold fast the inheritance of our fathers." Only for Jaffa, which had never been Jewish, and for Gezer did he offer compensation, in the sum of a hundred talents. Thus, though his argument was not wholly consistent, he opposed an historical claim to the land of his fathers to the King's title in law.

Antiochus VII was occupied with the campaign against Tryphon and so at first was able only to dispatch one of his officers as commander of the coastal area to prevent further expansion on the part of the Jews. His general Cendebaieus made Jabneh his base of operations and built the fortress of Kedron (now the village Katra) between Jabneh and Ashdod. From these bases he made incursions into Jewish territory; these were met more or less successfully by the Maccabees, and avenged by counterincursions. It was not until the summer of 134, after the death of Simon (who was murdered in February by his own son-in-law), that Antiochus VII personally led his army against Jerusalem, where in the meantime John (Yohanan) Hyrcanus, the son and heir of Simon, had assumed the rule. As always, the Jewish levy broke down in the face of the professional army of the King. By November Antiochus stood before Jerusalem and directed its siege. A double trench now cut off Jerusalem from all approach. Following a customary practice in ancient sieges, Hyrcanus expelled noncombatants from the Holy City in order to reduce the number of mouths that had to be fed. For the same reason Antiochus sent them back, and they wandered back and forth between the two armies. It was not until the Feast of Tabernacles in the fall of 133 that Hyrcanus received them back into the city. He also requested a seven days' truce of Antiochus because of the festival. Antiochus consented and even sent sacrificial animals, which were naturally wanting in the beleaguered city. In this manner negotiations were initiated. Hyrcanus was forced to capitulate. In the negotiations, however, the King confirmed the autonomy of the Jews and the position of Hyrcanus; but the walls of Jerusalem were pulled down. Hyrcanus was required to provide hostages, pay tribute, and yield up all the conquests of the Maccabees outside Judea. Even Gezer was taken from him. In 130 he was required to accompany the King upon his Parthian campaign with a Jewish levy. The achievement of Jonathan and Simon seemed to have been destroyed at a single blow. Jerusalem was again a dependent city, as in the days of Epiphanes and

Demetrius I. But now the High Priest was not of the legitimate house, but was a grandson of that Mattathias who, thirty years previously, had begun the insurrection against the great-uncle of Antiochus VII.

# JUDEA A HELLENISTIC PRINCEDOM

## JOHN HYRCANUS

———

Antiochus VII fell in his Parthian campaign (129 B.C.E.). A new epoch of confusion in the succession began in the Seleucid empire. The pretenders were now entirely without authority; each city and each tyrant pursued his own policy. The period of veering and tacking, the period of the tactics of Jonathan and Simon, was at an end. Upon the throne of the Maccabees now sat the representative of a new generation, John Hyrcanus, whose Greek name was apparently Alexander. He was born after the period of the persecutions; it was later thrown up to him that his mother had been a war captive under Epiphanes, and that her marriage to the priest Simon had therefore not been permissible. He was only a child when his uncle Jonathan became High Priest in the fall of 152. That he would obtain power was thus for him a foregone conclusion. Under his father he had been governor of Gezer. But the religious war, the struggle against the reform party, the hatred of the Greek oppressor—all that had inspired the sons of Mattathias, despite everything, to the end of their days—seemed to him strange and remote.

John Hyrcanus became a Hellenistic prince like his contemporaries and rivals, Zeno Cotylas in Rabbath Ammon (modern Amman) in Trans-Jordan, Erotimus, King of the Nabateans, and others. Each of them strove to expand his domain without troubling in the least about the Seleucids. Hyrcanus too became fully independent of the Seleucids; "Neither as subject nor as friend did he yield them aught." Unlike his uncle and his father, Hyrcanus wished to stand entirely upon his own feet.

But for this the first requisite was an effective army. The Jewish levy was as incompetent in the plain—particularly against the professional armies recruited from the Grecized cities of the coast—as it was superior in its native hills. How were these primitively armed Jewish shepherds to stand against the heavily armed horse and foot of the professional armies when the scene of battle was transferred to the level country "where there is neither stone nor flint, nor any place to flee unto"? But John wished to regain the plain and the coastal regions which he had lost in the peace pact of 133, and now there was no pretender to the throne whose protection could open the gates of the Greek cities to him. He had to organize a professional army, and that meant that he must recruit foreign soldiers. Immediately after the peace of 133, so it is said, in order to procure funds to hire mercenaries he opened the tomb of David and removed the treasures allegedly hidden there. This put an end to the popular period of the Maccabean monarchy. The prince now possessed an armed force alien to the people and obedient to him alone.

With these mercenaries, supplemented, of course, by native levies, Hyrcanus succeeded within twenty-five years in raising Judea to the position of the most significant military power in Syria. The course of his conquests is little known. He may have suffered frequent setbacks. We learn from two Roman documents of the period, for example, that in 132 the Jews sought Roman intervention to procure the restoration "of Jaffa, the harbors [that is, the landing places between Jabneh and Gaza], Gezer, Pegae, and other of their cities and localities which Antiochus had taken by force of arms contrary to the decree of the Senate." The reference was to the war against Antiochus VII. But about 110 we find them again complaining in Rome that Antiochus IX "had taken their fortresses and harbors and land." Soon Hyrcanus succeeded in winning back these "harbors," and the Jews besought the Roman Senate for protection "for their land and their harbors."

All this makes it plain how spirited was the struggle between the Jews and their opponents for access to the Mediterranean. At the turn of the century, in any case, the Jews were firmly established on the coast. Hyrcanus' realm extended as far north as Carmel. He was able to subjugate the hated Samaritans, and destroyed their temple on Mount Gerizim. Galilee was incorporated in the princedom and assigned as residence to Alexander Jannaeus, the younger son of Hyrcanus. In the south the Idumeans were subjugated. They accepted circumcision and the Torah and soon became complete Jews. When Hyrcanus died he left his son and successor, Judah Aristobulus, a territory which stretched from the north of Galilee to Masada, and from the sea to the Jordan.

Aristobulus reigned for only one year (104 to 103), and was succeeded by his brother, Alexander Jannaeus. Jannaeus continued his father's policy and waged incessant war against the neighboring cities and princes. At his death (76 B.C.E.) the entire coast, with the exception of Ascalon, from the border of Egypt to Carmel was under his sway. He won

Trans-Jordan, which at that time contained numerous flourishing Greek settlements. "The land between Gaza and Lebanon is called Judea," wrote a Greek geographer of the time. Palestine, "from Dan to Beersheba," was Jewish again. The biblical prophecies of happiness and prosperity seemed to have been fulfilled. But they were realized after Judea had become a Hellenistic princedom, and, after Aristobulus, a Hellenistic kingdom. It was this that provided the strength with which to conquer, but it was also this that was the inward reason for the dissolution of the new realm.

GENESIS AND CHARACTER

OF MACCABEAN HELLENISM

# GENESIS AND CHARACTER

## OF MACCABEAN HELLENISM

———

Today it is possible for us to observe the process of
Hellenization in individual features only. But these
features are sufficiently significant to enable those
who wish and are able to do so, to grasp the unity
of the historical reality.

A first indication of "assimilation" is the accommodation of proper names to the taste of the surrounding world. The leaders of the reform party
called themselves Jason instead of Jeshu, Menelaus
instead of Onias; the real name of the High Priest
Alcimus was Jakim. The Maccabees, on the other
hand, bore purely Hebrew names. Mattathias, son
of Yohanan, son of Simon, called his children
Yohanan (John), Simon, Judah, Eleazar, Jonathan.
His companions in the struggle were called Joseph,
Azariah, Mattathias, Judah. When emissaries were
to be sent to Rome, to be sure, they had to be persons
fluent in Greek, and they bore such names as Jason

and Eupolemus. But already Simon's son-in-law was called Ptolemaeus, and the sons of John Hyrcanus, Simon's grandson, had double names, Aristobulus-Judah, Alexander Jannaeus (*Yannay*, a short form of Jonathan). John Hyrcanus and Aristobulus struck their coins only in Hebrew; Jannaeus' coins are bilingual, bearing "King Jonathan" in Hebrew and "King Alexander" in Greek.

These coins were struck about 100 B.C.E. But forty years earlier, when the struggle with the Seleucids was still being waged, the Maccabees, who are customarily regarded as the bitter enemies and destroyers of Hellenistic culture, proclaimed the adherence of the Jewish people to the Hellenistic world. This took place in 143, under the High Priest Jonathan.

From the time of Alexander the Great, Greeks had been masters of the East. It was natural that the peoples and tribes of the East endeavored, by means of more or less skilfully contrived genealogical constructions, to attach themselves to the Greek people and to profess a kinship with them. Such a connection constituted, as it were, a ticket of admission to European culture. Thus, for example, the Pisidian city of Selge and the Lydian settlement of Cibyra in Caria, both mixed "barbarian" settlements in south-west Asia Minor, declared themselves to be Spartan colonies. In the year 126-125 Phoenician Tyre officially informed the Delphians of their kinship with them. Such derivations were promoted and facilitated by the tendencies of Greek science to link all new peoples, more or less naively, with those already known. The medieval practice of fitting newly discovered races into the framework of the biblical roll of nations (Gen. 10) is analogous. On the basis of an ingenious combination Greek scholarship had contrived a connection between the Jews and the Spartans. This was known as early as about 170 B.C.E. When Jason, the leader of the reform party, was ousted by Menelaus, he fled to Sparta and there claimed hospitality on the grounds of tribal kinship.

But as soon as the Maccabee Jonathan, who had so unexpectedly risen to be High Priest and chief of Jewry, was firmly in the saddle, he sent an embassy to Sparta (about 143) to renew the ancestral bond of brotherhood. His missive to "his brother Spartans" is extant. In it Jonathan refers to a letter of a Spartan king to "Onias the High Priest," and he subjoins a copy of this letter. The Spartan letter is a patent forgery, fabricated by some writer in Jonathan's service. In the spirit of the cosmopolitan philosophy of the period the Spartans are represented as saying to the Jews: "Your cattle and your possessions are ours, and ours are yours." But most important, the alleged Spartan declares that "in a writing concerning the Spartans and the Jews, the statement is made that they are brothers and, indeed, of the race of Abraham."

The forgery is not very skilful, but it is perfectly consonant with the spirit of the time. Men were eager to "discover" ancient evidence as a basis for the most recent friendships. But in all the forgeries and fictions of this class it is always the barbarians who claim a Hellenic descent: Romulus, the founder of Rome, is descended from Aeneas, a hero of the Iliad. It is significant of the Jewish forgery that the relationship is reversed: the Spartans are connected with the biblical patriarch.

Here the character and significance of Maccabean Hellenism is plainly revealed. The reform party wished to assimilate the Torah to Hellenism; the Maccabees wished to incorporate Hellenic culture in the Torah. The process was like that of the Europeanization of Japan: Japan possessed scholars who wrote about Botticelli and scientists who made bacteriological discoveries, but at the same time it could proclaim the Mikado's divine right of sovereignty on the ground of his direct descent from the goddess of the sun.

This accommodation of new elements to the Bible, this consideration for native tradition, characterizes the Hellenization carried through under the Maccabees, and differentiates it from the rationalistic assimilation which had been the aim of the reform party. Let us consider, for example, the decree of 140 B.C.E., by which the people invested Simon with the rulership. The document is thoroughly Hellenistic in character. It must have been drafted in Greek. In any case, the form is altogether that of a Greek honorary decree, utterly impossible in Hebrew. A long-winded and awkward period sets forth the reasons for the decree, and the decree itself is then expressed in an appended sentence. The very notion of drawing up a document to establish a constitution is purely Greek; the Bible provides no pattern for this. According to Hebrew models one would expect a general obligation of the people to Simon by means of an oath. But in this very document, which prohibits the wearing of purple or of the gold brooch which are the insignia of Hellenistic royalty, which offers Simon the rule out of gratitude for his deeds and in which he accepts it, a sharp distinction is nevertheless drawn between the privileged priesthood and the people; and rule is secured to Simon with the limitation, "until a faithful prophet shall arise." Only a divine revelation, not an assembly of the people, could proclaim eternal law for Israel.

Let us glance for a moment at Jonathan's letter to the Spartans. It is his desire to make known the kinship of the Jews with this Greek people. But at the same time he emphasizes that "the holy Scriptures we possess bring comfort to the Jews, and the help of Heaven delivers the Jews out of the hand of their enemies." Naively, he informs the Spartans that the Jews will remember them in their prayers, "as proper duty requires that brothers be remembered." We may imagine that the Spartans were somewhat puzzled by this missive. Their reply contains only a diplomatically courteous acknowledgment.

A third example. In antiquity as today, a proper legal title was sought for every conquest. Greek opinion held that the original legitimate owners of a territory might maintain a permanent claim upon it if it had been wrested from them by force. Thus the opponents of the Maccabees in the Greek cities of Phoenicia and Palestine maintained at the time of the Maccabean conquest that the Jews could have no claim upon Palestine because they were immigrants who had destroyed the Canaanites: "Are ye not a people of robbers?" It is of the highest significance for the Hellenization of Judaism under the Maccabees that the Jews engaged in this dispute without objection, that is to say, they recognized Greek opinion as arbiter in the case. Thus, it is important to note, they accepted the legal principle of their opponents. Whereas the Bible eschews any secular legal basis for the claim upon the land and derives the Jews' right to Canaan from the divine promise, under the Maccabees the Jews sought a historical basis for their claim to the Holy Land. But, and this is characteristic of the manner of their Hellenization, they applied this new principle to the Bible. They declared, for example, that Palestine originally belonged to the heritage of Shem and had then been occupied by Canaan in robber-fashion; or they identified Shem with Melchizedek, the priest-king of Jerusalem, thus seeking to prove that Palestine was Shem's heritage; or they employed some similar device. But it did not occur to them, for instance, to follow the Greek historian Hecataeus and dismiss all the charges of their opponents with the claim that Palestine was completely uninhabited at the time of the Jewish immigration. In territorial

91

disputes of this nature the Greeks always cited the writings of the historians, ancient documents, and similar sources, or even Homer; if one party to a quarrel found that some passage in the document to which it was appealing did not suit its argument, it declared that the offending passage had been interpolated. The Jews took over the Greek manner of argumentation, but for them the only source of knowledge remained the sacred Scripture, even when its evidence was against them.

The accommodation of Hellenistic civilization to the Torah, begun by the Maccabees and carried forward under their rule, gave Judaism the form that it was to have for centuries and that, in part, prevailed until the Emancipation. Judaism of the post-Maccabean period is Pharisaic. But Pharisaism, which is first mentioned in the period of John Hyrcanus, who was a disciple of the Pharisees, is in part characterized precisely by the introduction of certain leading ideas of the Hellenistic period into the world of the Torah.

The Pharisees or *perushim,* as they are designated in Hebrew, are the "Separated" who stand apart from the pagans and also from other Jews in order to gain sanctity. For them *parush* becomes a synonym for *kadosh,* "holy." They are not the only ones who separated themselves. The Essenes, another sect, who seem to have introduced something of the ideas and the forms of life of Greek Pythagoreanism into Judaism, desired to be "holy" no less than the Pharisees, and their striving in this direction was even more pronounced than the Pharisees'. But the Essenes sought to realize their goal for themselves alone, for the members of their own order; the Pharisees, on the other hand, wished to embrace the whole people, and in particular through education. It was their desire and intention that everyone in Israel achieve holiness through the study of the Torah, and their guiding principle was: "Raise up many disciples."

All of this is alien to biblical Israel. The prophets looked forward to repentance as issuing from the pressure of events and as a result of prophetic admonitions and divine chastisement, not as the fruit of study. Even for Jesus Sirach, who wrote his Book of Wisdom on the eve of the persecutions of Epiphanes, the scholar is a distinguished man and a rich one. An artisan or peasant, in his view, could not attain learning. "He that hath little business," he says, "can become wise. How can he become wise that holdeth the goad?" But the Pharisees wished to bring everyone to the Torah. "The crown of the

Torah is set before every man." For Sirach, as for biblical Judaism, as indeed for all the East, it is assumed that only the pious can be wise: "All wisdom cometh from the Lord." The Pharisees adopted this principle entirely, adding to it, however, that piety was teachable and to be attained only through teaching. Consequently the entire people must study the Torah.

But this is a Hellenic, one might say, a Platonic notion, that education could so transform the individual and the entire people that the nation would be capable of fulfilling the divine task set it. Hellenism introduces the first epoch of general popular education in the Occident. The Hellenes and the Grecized Orientals assembled in the gymnasia that were everywhere to be found and that served at once as athletic fields, schools, and clubs. In late Hellenistic Alexandria, as in the Greek community of the reform party in Jerusalem, the rights of citizenship were granted only after a sort of "proficiency test" was passed.

The Pharisees adopted these ideas and tendencies of the Hellenistic world, in that they associated the public sermons that had been customary since the time of Ezra with the teaching of the Torah. But it was not their ideal to fashion a Greek *kalos kai agathos,* or "gentleman," but to fulfil the precept which introduces the revelation on Sinai: "Ye shall be unto Me a kingdom of priests, and a holy nation."

To become a holy nation, indeed, was a goal common to all the Jews. But the Pharisees differed from the others by seeking its achievement through education and by not limiting this education to the Torah of Moses; they added many precepts wanting in the Torah, as, for example, the rule of washing the hands before meat. Any law written down naturally needs to be added to, and affords room for interpretation. One sect of Judaism in the Maccabean period, the Sadducees, wished to limit the laws to those expressly contained in the Torah. If something was neither prescribed nor forbidden in the Torah, they did not wish to make it so. Their principle was: "Only what is written is authoritative." But the Pharisaic idea of education promoted the tendency to develop the Torah as time and circumstance demanded. As the source for such development, the Pharisees looked to tradition, or, as they later termed it, the "oral" law, which they set on a footing with the written Torah. This singular notion of setting traditional usage or *halakhah* alongside the written law is again Greek. It is the concept of the "unwritten law" (*agraphos nomos*), which is preserved not on stone or paper but lives and moves in the actions of the people. But whereas in the Greek world this notion often served to negate the written law, Pharisaism used the oral law to "make a fence for the Torah."

In this way Maccabean Hellenism succeeded in parrying spiritual movements which might otherwise have destroyed traditional Judaism. For example, the Hellenistic world surrounding Judaism was caught up by a new revelation that solved the problem of evil on earth: retribution would come after death, when the wicked would be punished and the righteous rewarded and awakened to new life. Such notions are alien to the Bible, indeed in contradiction to it, for the Torah promises reward and punishment in this life. Hence the Sadducees rejected the new doctrine and ridiculed the Pharisaic teaching of resurrection. If they had been the only authoritative representatives of Judaism, Judaism would either have lagged behind the times and grown rigid, as was the case with the Samaritans, who also rejected the new belief, or the course of history would have submerged Judaism and undermined the Torah. The Pharisees, on the other hand, adopted the Hellenistic doctrine of resurrection, but subsumed it under the principles of the Torah.

What to the pagans was an event dictated more or less by necessity, appears among the Jews as the working of the free will of God. According to the account of Flavius Josephus, the Pharisaic doctrine of the future life derives from the Greek teaching of the Pythagoreans. But among the Pythagoreans each soul must automatically return to new life after death, each according to its merit. For this fateful and continually operative necessity, the Pharisees substituted the single event of the Last Judgment, whose day and scope God would determine, and so dovetailed the new Hellenistic idea into the structure of biblical ideas. In its new form the adopted doctrine of resurrection developed into a characteristic element of Jewish belief; it became, with biblical monotheism, its central doctrine. The Jewish prayer book still reads: "Praised be Thou, Lord our God and God of our fathers, God of Abraham, God of Isaac, and God of Jacob. . . . Thou art mighty for eternity, O Lord, Thou quickenest the dead."

# FROM ALEXANDER JANNAEUS

## TO POMPEY

———

The Pharisees wished to make over the entire people of Israel into their own image—they wished to make of Israel, as the command on Sinai prescribed, "a holy nation." In consequence, they came forward with such comprehensive claims as no party either before or after them had done. In the house as upon the street, every movement of the pious was regulated. The Pharisees prescribed that no knot might be tied or loosed on the Sabbath, but they also prescribed the cases in which this rule might admit of exceptions. For example, a woman might tie the strings of her bonnet on a Saturday. So comprehensive a concept of the life of a people is only possible when and because the people are in full agreement with the dominant belief. At the time of Flavius Josephus—that is to say, at the time of the destruction of the Temple by the Romans (70 C.E.)—the spiritual unity of party and people had been attained. Although the Pharisees had no constitutional means of enforcing discipline, Josephus tells us, they possessed such influence that the people concurred with them even when they spoke against King or High Priest. All acts of worship, prayers as well as sacrifices, were carried out according to their ordinances. Even the Sadducees, whenever they obtained official positions, were obliged to keep to what the Pharisees laid down, however irksome and constraining they might find it, for otherwise they would not be tolerated by the people. It was about the year 100 that the Pharisees made their bid for spiritual domination over Israel, and their comprehensive claims necessarily developed into a conflict with the Maccabees. The ideal state, Plato declared, cannot come into being unless kings become philosophers or philosophers kings. The Pharisees were confronted with the same dilemma: the Maccabees must either become Pharisees or give way to the Pharisees.

According to our sources, the vicissitudes of the conflict between the state and the religious movement developed somewhat as follows: John Hyrcanus (134 to 104) was at first a friend and disciple of the Pharisees. He permitted them to lay their commands and prohibitions upon the people. Later he turned from them, allegedly because he was personally offended by a Pharisee. "He forbade observance of their regulations on pain of punishment, and joined the Sadducees. In consequence the hatred of the people was turned upon him and his sons."

The Pharisees of the period of 100 B.C.E. must not be imagined according to the pattern of the peace-loving teachers of Jabneh who were preaching harmony two centuries later. Early Pharisaism was a belligerent movement that knew how to hate.

When Alexander Jannaeus was defeated by the Arabs about 90 B.C.E. he fled to Jerusalem. This military reverse, as is often the case, afforded the enemies of the government opportunity to agitate. Civil strife began, and lasted for six years. When Jannaeus asked the insurgents what they wished, they replied, his death. Against this great-grandson of Mattathias they invited the assistance of one of the last of the Seleucids, Demetrius III. The armies met at Shechem. Demetrius urged Jannaeus' mercenaries to make common cause with him, the Hellene; and Jannaeus, for his part, sought to move the Jews who were with Demetrius to desert. Demetrius won. Jannaeus' mercenaries were annihilated. But sympathy

103

for the defeated Jews caused a portion of Demetrius' Jewish allies to desert the pagan victor. Demetrius retired from the country and Jannaeus was enabled to suppress the insurrection. In Jerusalem he celebrated his triumph in a carousal with his concubines. In their presence he set up eight hundred crosses on which to nail the captive rebels, whose wives and children were slaughtered before their eyes.

It is not easy to determine whether the insurrection was the work of the Pharisees or whether other elements exploited for their own purposes the dissatisfaction fanned by the Pharisees. A pregnant sentence of Jannaeus' is preserved in the Talmud: "Fear neither the Pharisees nor those who are not Pharisees, but only the painted ones who resemble Pharisees." Whatever the case may have been, the Pharisees later persecuted the counselors of Jannaeus.

But this was under a new regime. Upon his deathbed (76 B.C.E.) Jannaeus transferred the royal dignity to his wife, Salome Alexandra, and is said to have advised her himself to alter the government's policy. She named her eldest son, Hyrcanus II, High Priest, and entrusted the government to the hands of the Pharisees. Those ordinances of the time of Hyrcanus which had fallen into desuetude were again put into force. Alexandra ruled in title only; the real power was in the hands of the Pharisees.

Having come into power, the Pharisees took vengeance upon the counselors of Jannaeus—who had recommended the crucifixion of the captives—by executing them. How did the Pharisees control the machinery of state? It appears that Alexandra introduced the scribes into the Sanhedrin, or council of state, where previously only the chief priests and members of the lay nobility had sat. Thus it was possible for the Pharisees, under the leadership of Simon ben Shetah, to employ the might of the state to overwhelm their opponents.

The anti-Pharisaic opposition consolidated itself under Alexandra and her second son, Aristobulus. As soon as the Queen died (67 B.C.E.) open war broke out between Aristobulus and his brother, Hyrcanus II, the legitimate successor. Aristobulus won. Hyrcanus renounced the throne, but soon sought to regain the crown with the help of the Arab Nabateans, to whom he promised to restore certain of the conquests of Jannaeus. His confidant and instigator in this struggle was Antipater the Idumean, father of the future King Herod. In the spring of 65 Aristobulus, occupying the Temple Mount, was besieged by Hyrcanus and his Arab allies and negotiations were under way concerning the price of sacrificial victims that were necessary for the service in the Sanctuary.

But in the meantime the map of the world changed. Rome, which had long looked upon events in the East with indifference, was aroused by the conquests of King Mithridates of Pontus. In 66 Pompey defeated the Pontic king and also vanquished the Armenian Tigranes who then ruled Syria. When Pompey's legate Scaurus came to Damascus, he heard of the war between the brothers in Jerusalem. Scaurus hastened thither, and his expectations were realized. Both parties offered him money. He decided in favor of Aristobulus. The word of the Roman was sufficient cause for the Arabs to raise the siege.

But Scaurus was only the forerunner of one greater. In the spring of 63 Pompey himself came to Damascus. Again the Jewish parties appeared before him. Pompey postponed his decision. But Aristobulus feared that Pompey might in the end pronounce for Hyrcanus, who was supported by a numerous Jewish embassy. By his awkward conduct Aristobulus quickly lost the confidence of Pompey, who now ordered the occupation of Jerusalem. Aristobulus' supporters refused to admit the Romans,

106

but the party of Hyrcanus opened the gates of the city to them. The troops of Aristobulus, who had in the meanwhile been made captive by Pompey, again assembled on the Temple Mount. Pompey, supported by Hyrcanus, began the siege. In the fall of 63 the fortress was stormed and its defenders subdued. But even in the midst of the slaughter the priests continued the sacrificial service at the altar according to rule, paying no regard to the fury of the civil strife. They were struck down by the Romans at the very altar.

The proper history of the Maccabees thus comes to an end. Judea became a vassal princedom of the Romans. Hyrcanus II was at its head, no longer as king, however, but only as High Priest. As such, he lost the entire non-Jewish part of his realm, the acquisitions of Hyrcanus I and of Jannaeus. His princedom still included Judea, Samaria, Galilee, and Idumea, but was completely cut off from the sea by the coast cities liberated by Pompey. Most of Trans-Jordan too was lost to the Jews. Then in 40 B.C.E. Hyrcanus II was overthrown by the Parthians, led by his nephew Antigonus. Three years later Antigonus too was vanquished by the Romans, and Antipater's son Herod was entrusted with the rule of Judea. Herod married Mariamne (Miriam), a grand-

107

daughter of Hyrcanus II, and in 35 he made her brother Aristobulus High Priest; but in the following year he had him killed. In 30 he also caused the execution of the aged Hyrcanus, who since his fall from power had been living in Jerusalem as a private citizen. In the next year he also killed Mariamne, thinking she had been unfaithful to him. Next came the turn of Mariamne's mother, Alexandra. In 25 he caused the distant relatives of Hyrcanus to be tracked down and killed. Thus the last remnant of the house of the Hasmoneans was destroyed.

Historians since Flavius Josephus have been wont to ascribe the fall of the house to intestine strife. "Hyrcanus and Aristobulus were responsible for this disaster to Jerusalem. Therefore have we lost our liberty, and become subject to Rome." Others maintain that upon Alexandra "falls the responsibility for the rapid loss of the rule that had been achieved with such toil and danger," because she ruled according to the will of the enemies of the house, the Pharisees, repelling the true friends of the dynasty. This is obviously naive. When Pompey had once appeared in Syria, the subjugation of Jerusalem was inevitable. Rather, the quarrel between Hyrcanus and Aristobulus saved Jerusalem from disaster. For now the Romans appeared in Judea as allies of at least one of the Jewish parties.

It was more important that Pharisaism had led to an estrangement of the people from the dynasty. Before Pompey at Damascus there appeared an embassy of Jews, who set forth to him that Rome had long been the protector of the Jews, who had thus enjoyed autonomy. Their head had been a High Priest, not a king. Their present Maccabean rulers, they declared, had enslaved the people and destroyed their ancestral constitution; they maintained their position only by terror and by the support of their soldiery. Later and in a precisely similar fashion, after the death of Herod, the Jews petitioned that none of the Herodians be named king, but that they be permitted to live without a king, according to the law of their fathers.

It is easy to see that the consistent Pharisees would sympathize with this position. To them it must have appeared that a foreign domination respecting Jewish autonomy and recognizing the Torah as the binding law of Judaism would offer less hindrance to their work of education. Precisely because it was foreign, and hence concerned only for the prompt payment of tribute and for civil order, they assumed that the internal life of the people would remain outside the range of its interest. According to Josephus, the people once pelted Alexander Jannaeus at the Feast of Tabernacles with *etrogim* (citrons), which are used in the ritual of that festival, because, as the son of a mother who had been a war captive, he was deemed unworthy of the priestly dignity. This objection was in keeping with the Pharisaic interpretation of the ordinances for the marriage of priests (Lev. 21:7). The Pharisees might justly expect foreign rulers scrupulously to follow the opinions of the scholars in all such matters whereas a Jewish king, as was the case with the Maccabees, would desire to shape even the internal and religious life of the people according to his own notions and not always according to the recommendations of the teachers of the law. In point of fact, it was the Roman rule which made possible and facilitated the development of Pharisaic Judaism to a high degree, until the great conflict between the two unequal powers set in. In this conflict the Jewish people lost its land, in order to win a historic continuity such as was vouchsafed to no other people of antiquity, not even to their conquerors, the Romans.

Who will venture to decide at this date whether, during the crisis after the death of Alexandra, one

110

or the other of the Jewish political leaders was in the right? In the struggle between Aristobulus and Hyrcanus the partisans of the latter wished to have a wonder-worker named Honiah call down a solemn curse upon Aristobulus. But Honiah stepped forward between the contending parties and said: "O God, king of the universe, forasmuch as those standing about me are Thy people, but the besieged Thy priests, may it be Thy will neither to hearken to those against these, nor to fulfil what these pray against those." Can the historian of today judge otherwise than in the sense of this prayer concerning those who stood opposed to each other in hatred at the fall of the house of the Hasmoneans?

But the historian may deduce from the progress of history that precisely this estrangement of the people or its parts from the dynasty had great and, in the sequel, wholesome effects on Judaism. The subjugation of 63, by which the Jews again became subjects of an alien and pagan power, now no longer seemed a national and religious catastrophe that called forth despair for the future of the nation and the beneficence of God; rather, it seemed the just penalty for a dynasty of usurpers. In the apocryphal Psalms of Solomon, composed about this time, the Maccabees appear as wicked men who by violence

111

occupied a throne not theirs but promised by God to the anointed of the house of David. The shoot of David, the promised Messiah, would one day crush the rulers and drive the heathen out; but not by earthly means, as the Maccabees wrongly thought they could do, but by the hand of God. "Happy is he whose help is the God of Jacob."

With the end of the Hasmoneans the messianic period of Jewish history begins.

# CONCLUSION

———

The Maccabees saved Israel from the Greek danger. But this danger was twofold, and the Maccabees eradicated one kind of Hellenism only to facilitate the growth of another kind.

Hellenism was a supranational culture based upon reason and faith in reason. Hence its immediate effect upon all peoples whom it embraced was everywhere to disrupt tradition. If the Greek gymnasium in which naked youths indulged in sport was an abomination to the Maccabean Jew, in the same period the Elder Cato complains that the natural modesty of the Romans was being undermined by Greek athletic games; even during the Empire an old-fashioned Roman declares: "The relaxation of morals derives primarily from [Greek] cultivation of the body." In the Book of Maccabees the word "Hellenism" signifies "anti-Jewish." But in the Roman poet Plautus (died 184 B.C.E.) *pergraecari* ("to play the Greek") is virtually equivalent to "to be debauched." Cicero's grandfather used to say that the

113

better a Roman spoke Greek, the more certain was he a scoundrel.

Contact with the "enlightened" and universal culture of Hellenism could only be salutary for one who, wrestling as Jacob did with the angel, did not allow himself to be overcome but extorted its blessing, not losing himself in Hellenism, but coming safely away with enhanced strength. Only two peoples of antiquity succeeded in doing so, the Romans and the Jews. The Romans succeeded because they became the rulers even of the Hellenic world. To be sure, they lost much in the process, a good part of their national religion, for instance, whose gods Greek gods supplanted. The Jews succeeded because their knowledge of the oneness of God and of His world rule—in a word, the singular character of their faith —set up an inner barrier against surrender and separated them from the rest of the world.

But separation alone could by its nature only preserve past gains; it could not enrich the spirit and the inner life. Many other Oriental peoples, as for example the Egyptians, shut themselves off from Hellenism; but this led only to their becoming backward; and their leading classes, seduced by Hellenism, were lost to the nation.

Jerusalem had been threatened with a similar fate. The leading men of Jewry went over to a foreign culture. The world of Hellenism offered hospitality, and they joined it at table. But by its prescriptions concerning the sacred and the profane the Torah interfered with this elegant love feast. The leading social class in Jerusalem therefore determined to abolish the separateness of the Jewish religion and its religious way of life, and if necessary to employ force in order to transform Judaism into a "philosophic" form of paganism. This was the party of the "reformers."

The Maccabees protested. They defended the God of their fathers against the deity fabricated by the reformers. By their uprising they preserved the uniqueness and permanence of Judaism, and they preserved monotheism for the world. The victory and reign of the Maccabees (after 152 B.C.E.) put an end to anti-Jewish Hellenism forever.

But the question of a final settlement with Hellenism had not been resolved. Hellenism continued to be a universal spiritual power, like Western civilization in the modern world—no people could isolate itself from it if it wished to live and assert itself. Above all, isolation would have involved a break with the already numerous communities of the Diaspora, which were scattered throughout the Greek world and hence were constrained to accept Hellenism.

With the Maccabees, then, the internal Jewish reconcilement with Hellenism begins. Ideas and concepts of the new age and the new culture were taken over without thereby surrendering native spiritual values. This was managed in two ways. First, the inner strengthening of the people achieved by the Maccabees made it possible to adopt unaltered ideas and institutions which had previously seemed to offer, or in fact did offer, a serious threat. John Hyrcanus was unwilling to admit a Seleucid garrison into Jerusalem because it was impossible for Jews and foreigners to live together. But he himself raised an army of foreign mercenaries. At the time of Epiphanes the gymnasium in Jerusalem was enormously dangerous to Judaism. In the time of Philo the Jews of Alexandria thronged the games without sacrificing any part of Judaism; and the theater, amphitheater, and hippodrome erected in Jerusalem by Herod were later visited even by orthodox Jews.

Secondly, Hellenistic notions were appropriated only after their poison had been drawn. The recipe was very simple: the new was fitted into the system

116

of the Torah and was employed the better to serve the God of the fathers, not to elude Him the more adroitly. The sect of the Essenes, for example, which is mentioned as early as the turn of the second century B.C.E. and which was highly esteemed by the Jews, is a thoroughly Hellenistic growth upon Palestinian soil. In their organization, their moral practices, their usages, the Essenes imitated the Greek sect of the Pythagoreans. They even took it upon themselves to repudiate the sacrificial practices of the Temple. But all of this they subsumed under the Torah. They took the ancestral laws as their schoolmasters, zealously studied the Torah, honored Moses next to God, sent their offerings to the Temple, and in the Roman war accepted martyrdom rather than eat forbidden food.

Thus Judaism was able to enrich itself with new and foreign ideas and to be saved from the mummification that overtook the religion of the Egyptians, for example, which shut itself off from Hellenism completely. If today the West and Islam believe in resurrection, the idea is one which Maccabean Judaism took over from Hellenism and then passed on to Christianity and Islam.

The Maccabees preserved the Judaism of the Greek period from both dissolution and ossification.

117

It is through their deeds that the God of Abraham, Isaac, and Jacob could and did remain our God. "My help cometh from the Lord, who made heaven and earth" (Ps. 121:2).

———

The Maccabean kings made provision for their fame.
Under their patronage a history of the dynasty was
written in Hebrew (or Aramaic) towards the end of
the second century B.C.E. This chronicle was known
in Palestine as late as the fourth century of the Common Era. With the impoverishment of the Jews
during the decline of the Roman Empire, they gave
up copying all extraneous works and concentrated
upon the preservation of Scripture and Talmud. But
in the meantime the Christian Church appropriated
as its own the Jewish martyrs to the faith whose tri-
umphal death is recounted in the so-called Second
Book of Maccabees, written in Greek. Christian
copyists included this work in their Bible, where its
presence attracted a Greek translation of the Maccabean chronicle; this became the First Book of
Maccabees. Except for supplementary information
provided by Josephus or found in Greek and Roman
literature, our knowledge of Maccabean history derives from these two Books of Maccabees. Rabbinic

literature contains only scattered references to the subject.

Protestants accepted as inspired, and therefore as canonical, only the Old Testament books included in the Hebrew Bible, and sought to discredit the books of the Maccabees that Catholics recognized as part of Scripture. Polemics continued unabated until the end of the eighteenth century and later. But both antagonists were ignorant of the problems they endeavored to elucidate. In the fall of the Roman Empire pagans as well as Jews had to conserve their forces, and discarded the secondary parts of their spiritual armament. Thus works composed in Greek during the Maccabean age, that is, in the second and first centuries B.C.E., have disappeared almost completely. We have only inscriptions, papyri, and other monuments discovered within the last sixty or seventy years to enable us to place the Maccabees in their proper historical framework. The most recent scholarly commentary on the Books of Maccabees was published ninety years ago, and a historical interpretation of the Maccabean age remains to be written. The present essay is intended only as a nucleus for a future extended work on the subject.

# CHRONOLOGY

---

*Numerals in brackets refer to pages of this book*

330: Alexander the Great conquers the Persian Empire, including Palestine [22].

3rd Century: Palestine under the rule of the Ptolemies of Egypt.

200: Antiochus III of Syria conquers Palestine.

187–176: Seleucus IV Philopator. The Wisdom of Jesus the Son of Sirach.

176: Antiochus IV Epiphanes.

175–172: Jason as High Priest. Beginning of the Hellenization of Jerusalem [26].

172–163: Menelaus as High Priest.

169: First Egyptian campaign of Epiphanes. The Temple plundered.

168: Rome conquers Macedonia. World dominion of Rome established.

168: Second Egyptian campaign of Epiphanes. Founding of Acra in Jerusalem [27].

167 (end): Temple desecrated; beginning of the persecutions [13].

166: Uprising of Mattathias [16].

165: Judah succeeds to the leadership [35]. The Book of Daniel. Campaign of Lysias [39].

164 (spring): End of the persecutions. Epiphanes' amnesty [40].

164 (end): Temple dedication [42]. Inauguration of Hannukah [43].

163: Death of Epiphanes [45]. Campaign of Eupator. Defeat of Judah [47].

162 (beginning): Treaty of peace [48]. Alcimus as High Priest [51].

161: Judah's victory over Nicanor [54]. Judah's alliance with the Romans [55].

160 (spring): Death of Judah [57].

159: Death of High Priest Alcimus [63].

152 (fall): Jonathan as High Priest [63].

146: Destruction of Carthage by the Romans.

142 (end): Death of Jonathan [66]. Simon.

141 (spring): Conquest of Acra [67].

140: Simon as Ethnarch [68].

134: Death of Simon [71].

134–104: John Hyrcanus I [78].

134–133: Antiochus VII subdues Jerusalem but confirms its autonomy [72].

133: Beginning of the Gracchan revolution in Rome.

104–103: Aristobulus [80].

103–76: Alexander Jannaeus [80].

76–67: Salome Alexandra [104].

63: Pompey conquers Jerusalem [107].

# THE HOUSE OF THE MACCABEES (HASMONEANS)

## (167–29 B.C.E.)

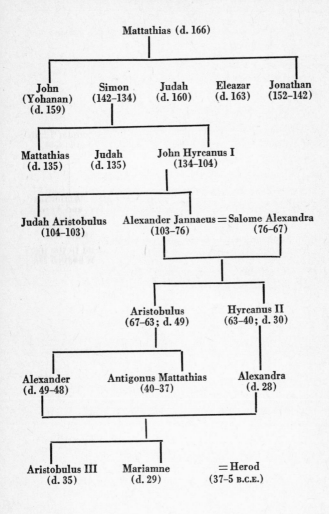

Mattathias (d. 166)

John (Yohanan) (d. 159) — Simon (142–134) — Judah (d. 160) — Eleazar (d. 163) — Jonathan (152–142)

Mattathias (d. 135) — Judah (d. 135) — John Hyrcanus I (134–104)

Judah Aristobulus (104–103) — Alexander Jannaeus (103–76) = Salome Alexandra (76–67)

Aristobulus (67–63; d. 49) — Hyrcanus II (63–40; d. 30)

Alexander (d. 49–48) — Antigonus Mattathias (40–37) — Alexandra (d. 28)

Aristobulus III (d. 35) — Mariamne (d. 29) = Herod (37–5 B.C.E.)

# THE SELEUCID KINGS
## IN THE TIME OF THE MACCABEES

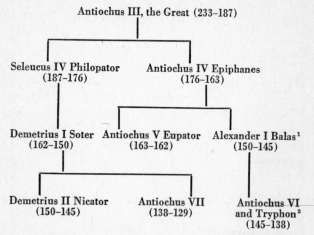

Antiochus III, the Great (233–187)

Seleucus IV Philopator (187–176)    Antiochus IV Epiphanes (176–163)

Demetrius I Soter (162–150)    Antiochus V Eupator (163–162)    Alexander I Balas[1] (150–145)

Demetrius II Nicator (150–145)    Antiochus VII (138–129)    Antiochus VI and Tryphon[2] (145–138)

[1] Balas passed himself off as Epiphanes' illegitimate son.

[2] Antiochus VI, while still a minor, was elevated to the throne by a man named Tryphon, who then waged war against Demetrius II in Antiochus' name.

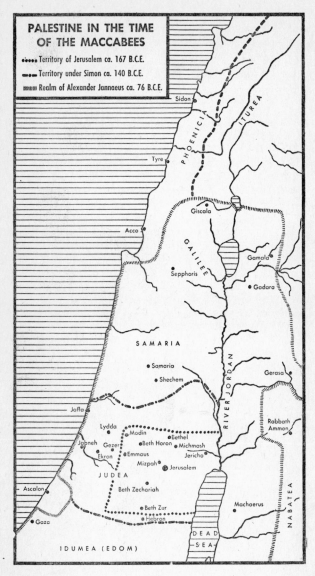

**PALESTINE IN THE TIME OF THE MACCABEES**

•••• Territory of Jerusalem ca. 167 B.C.E.

▬▬ Territory under Simon ca. 140 B.C.E.

▥▥▥ Realm of Alexander Jannaeus ca. 76 B.C.E.

Sidon

PHOENICIA

ITUREA

Tyre

Giscala

Acco

GALILEE

Gamala

Sepphoris

Gadara

SAMARIA

Samaria

Gerasa

Shechem

RIVER JORDAN

Jaffa

Lydda

Bethel

Modin

Rabbath Ammon

Beth Horon

Michmash

Jabneh

Gezer

Jericho

Ekron

Emmaus

Mizpah

Jerusalem

JUDEA

Beth Zechariah

NABATEA

Ascalon

Beth Zur

Machaerus

Hebron

Gaza

DEAD SEA

IDUMEA (EDOM)